Items should be returned on or befor
shown below. Items not already requ
borrowers may be renewed in perso.,
telephone. To renew, please quote the number on the
barcode label. To renew online a PIN is required.
This can be requested at your local library.
Renew online @ **www.dublincitypubliclibraries.ie**
Fines charged for overdue items will include postage
incurred in recovery. Damage to or loss of items will
be charged to the borrower.

Leabharlanna Poiblí Chathair Bhaile Átha Cliath
Dublin City Public Libraries

Baile Átha Cliath
Dublin City

Brainse Rátheanaigh
Raheny Branch
Tel: 8315521

D1137813

Date Due	Date Due	Date Due

Also by THOMAS MCCARTHY

Poetry
The First Convention · 1978
The Sorrow Garden · 1981
The Non-Aligned Storyteller · 1984
Seven Winters in Paris · 1989
The Lost Province · 1996
Mr Dineen's Careful Parade · 1999
Merchant Prince · 2005
The Last Geraldine Officer · 2009

Novels
Without Power · 1991
Asya and Christine · 1992

Non-Fiction
Gardens of Remembrance · 1998
Rising from the Ashes · 2010

Thomas McCarthy

Pandemonium

CARCANET

First published in Great Britain in 2016 by

CARCANET PRESS LTD

Alliance House, 30 Cross Street

Manchester M2 7AQ

www.carcanet.co.uk

A CIP catalogue record for this book is available

from the British Library, ISBN 9781784102968.

Book design: Luke Allan.

Printed & bound in England by SRP Ltd.

The publisher acknowledges financial assistance

from Arts Council England.

CONTENTS

PANDEMONIUM

for Peter Jay

Thank you for your recent letter, Dennis O'Driscoll.
This is just a brief note before all the others rush in,
Rush in with their first response to the bleak quotation
You offered us on Christmas Eve. The earliest mail

Will set the record straight: let pandemonium
Cease, let the wild confetti of poets
Be withdrawn from the bitterness of the streets.
Let me put it simply, your last fine poem

Was more than any editor expected. It frightened
The life out of all who read to the bitter end,
Not anticipating such a turn of phrase. I suspend
My judgement, still, and hope you may yet lighten

Those closing words. Dennis, all quotation marks
I would remove for now – as things stand,
You don't need to hide behind another poet's hand
Or ventriloquise your long-suffering heart.

Life is a dry skull, it's true. Death is
A ruthless and obsessive boss,
But you were too smart to take mere dictation
In any departure lounge or railway station.

In truth, dear correspondent, your loss is our loss
And your absence is more than a lost quotation –
Which is why I'll bring this note from station to station
To catch you between trains, at Thurles or Charing Cross.

The land is not yet settled
After our years of pandemonium.
This time it is almost too late
To sing with full heart a parting hymn,
Or indulge in the usual fickle
Humour of things. It is too late

To bolt the door of Ireland.
A penny candle struggles in the wind,
A corpse from the West rises
To face me. What was a house now stands
As a ghost from the assizes.
Believe me, I tried to understand

All the signals we received from Berlin.
Little did they know, in our autonomous
Region all the gold was gorse,
And all investment was storytelling.
Blackbirds in the oak trees are trembling still
Where all our demons hurriedly went in.

THE HOPE OF FINDING SOMETHING

i.m. Seamus Heaney

What a fool I am to be going into this new bookshop,
Knowing that our poet is dead. The happiness of youth
And all its insatiable dreams, the first book I could afford,
The first kiss, the first breast, the first summer night
To fall asleep with someone in my arms, the first words
She spoke to me were his. She didn't want me to stop

Listening and I didn't want the long summer to stop.
She pointed exactly to where I never wished to go,
Having lately escaped from an oppression of such fields:
I did not wish to return to where I was nothing. So
Adamant was her love for his new books I baulked
At the very thought of attachment. Now I know

The true weight of love, what it's ordinary to know
In a secured home, in a freehold with boundaries –
Back then I couldn't tell. Back then I was too alone
With social resentment, and cut too far adrift,
To catch the subtlety of his bogs and blackberries.
I had missed the ordinary and its tectonic shift

Within Irish life. Strong as Ireland in her makeshift
Tent, she knew words were about her and not about him,
However much she loved his vowel sounds. Sing, sing
Like Ulster, she said, but go and find your own theme.
I saw her by his coffin as it passed. Now that we're cut adrift,
I'll try this bookshop in the hope of finding something.

The plover and the plover's page
Apply their narceine to Kenmare water

In this, the earliest light of wintertime.
Night lifts its bitter crystalline,

Clouds withdraw in wounded hauteur.

Sunlight tinctures sorrel and sage
With drifts of its royal orpiment

While we gaze upon a lobster boat
As it drops a rosary-beads of pots.

Gulls attend each sinking reliquary,
Chattering classes in a frenzy of prayer –

The hour is so casually strummed upon,
It booms in opiate languor:

This sun is a river, the plover's a sea.

I watch the timeless candle burning at both ends.
At one end it must be my mother's face
And her infinite correlation with my own fate.
There's no other end that I would put in place

At this moment or at any moment in our room.
The candle burns in its circadian rhythms,
Leaving words behind it on her waxy lips:
She told stories to the dark while the world slept

And like poems she didn't need an end
But supped off the oils of perpetual change.
I watch the warm light on your own restless face.
You are restless like a mother. The precipice

Of night threatens you, though I am here
Always to hold you. You must learn to un-drown
Yourself, to float the way light does
From a timeless candle. Your superstition grows

In the absence of day, but night has no substance
When we are together. Look at the stars
Through the bedroom window: their universe
Is nothing in this huge room, in the light from us.

Like us, the tide is seeking a cove
Where it doesn't need to be obliging. Love
In its secret cave may rise and fall
To its own moon: the beck and call
Of the sea won't be heard. The cliff face
Runs its mascara, such tears of disgrace

As leave the rocks with purple stains.
It is clear the sky has taken pains
To shoo such clouds away as might
Freckle the foreshore from a great height.
The tide's scandalous incompetence
Is complete: the sea runs out of patience

With every form of rock and pool –
This tide of love has never bent to any school
But ebbs in its own petulant way:
The way art or water does, you say;
The way all things that are fought for
Settle in a hidden cove and accept water.

Here on the writing desk of the earth
The sun goes down quickly at ink level.
Soon the stony outcrop will be a blob
Of light blue and the sky will be pale
As the tissue rises. Is it time to go in
Or is it time to go outside? Only time

Will tell me how the levels rise –
Phrases cluster on the sunlit page,
So many oyster-catchers thread the surf,
Their needlepoint becomes pale green.
Water is near, shale bursts in applause,
Gulls congregate on a drifting raft.

Am I going out or coming in with the sea?
Not everything is blessed by the promise
Of water: your book on birds
Is soaked by the wash, ink grows pale
In its buckled galleys. From the Hellespont
Of a paper clip, Leander swims to me.

Between the high water mark and low,
Early sun releases itself without permission;
The long shadows make a house for me,
Or the child I always carry: a house of sand.
Childhood like the seashore has no title.
Everything is lost in time's arraignment
As every begetter knows. The faucet of the ocean
Is running its green water, this bath
Is prepared for the child I never became.

Sandpipers cry: don't leave yours eggs
In another's nest. Here I walk on my own,
Like the gannet working up for a dive:
I am never going home. It is the sea
Feels sorry for itself, not for me,
As it speaks of personal immensities:
Here the drying sand and the wet part
Create a path through the heart. The ink
Trail that pain makes on the page is the

Blindness of a seabird going too deep.
When I turn to walk back I feel the chill
Of early morning on a manipulative face.
Footprints in the sand are only me
Walking eastward again. The sea-road
Changes and the sun gains confidence:
Memory is upright in the sky. Let me
Permit the high dive the gannet makes, the
Passage made by shadows, the bird's cry.

Pawns tumble on the backward surf
Against the atelier of my tent: it could be an opening

Or an endgame the way the winds are;
Or a princess in her blue gown: the treaty of

Her familiar perfume wants to wake me,
A promise of oakmoss, a tincture of myrrh

And all the iodine of her Highness.
I am far from the desert but not from the sand.

The sun rises like a stern king as seawater
Tries an opening; bold as vetiver, empowered as
A bishop in the long diagonal of the sea.

1. Shanbally Terrace

When they distributed life chances there were none
Left over for you. There were a few days of thinning beet
On Loobys' farm, there was a tree fallen in Chearnley's wood
That could be cut and sold, and if the sun shone
There was the long walk to Hogan's orchard. The height

Of luxury was a week or two in a Protestant garden.
It was difficult to reach poetry in a street like yours,
Though the themes were everywhere, so much refuse
Of life released from the pub, the overturned bin
Of each night; the smear of blood as if, in the dead hours,

A poet had been blackberry-picking. Such a leakage
Of geography in such a place: that is not your country,
That street, or if it is it must end at *The Railway Bar*
In Beggar's Bush or at Deptford, at the water's edge
Where a Waterford large bottle hits the North Sea.

It is cold there, apart from your mother's laughter:
There is something heroic in her, something detached
From your deeply, unremitting, practised despair.
She is buoyed by hauntings from another
World: a singer who sings her nonsense, a mother.

II. *The Bourgeois Class, 1964*

You have been sent here by your father to see O'Connors'
Brand new White House, a pearl in pebble-dash
Built for the newly-weds. It is something for the poor
To wonder at, a balsam for all the horrors
Of the Sixties. A nest. Your uncle turns with a flourish

And reads the riot act to all from Shanbally Terrace:
You must not enter without permission, you must not
Put fingers sticky from lollipops to the gate or door.
Your uncle has set himself up as a kind of secret police
On behalf of the respectable in Cappoquin. It is the lot

Of luckier families, he says, to own a business
Or practise behind brass plates. Your father,
Who runs his own private little soviet, demurs:
For him, wealth is an ignorant wilderness,
With blood on every premises and every acre.

But you side with your Uncle Mick as you walk together,
Collecting spare newspapers or swill from rich kitchens.
Cappoquin was your Camino de Compostela. Your pilgrim's chore
Was feeding pigs as you carried buckets in bad weather:
At each parlour you must have seemed both beggar and urchin.

Aristocracy in every land is a kind of grand theft,
Yet you loved to sit where the Brigadier had hidden
The stolen seventeenth century, and more –
Neither he nor you were here at all, you've left
For Rio de Janiero: you have bidden

Waterford goodbye. There is such a radiance
From his single drawing-room fire
You are really thieves already in tropical exile.
Now Alec Waugh's *Hot Countries* makes sense,
All that coconut, rum and desire
That makes of everywhere a sceptred isle.

Such theatre and evasion at the top of the glass:
You've always felt at home among those beautiful
Blackguards, the ones waiting for a refill of gin;
For the sake of style you would let everything pass.
The bravado and champagne, effortless idyll

Behind the walls of each Parthenon, seemed
Like a fitting use of each collapsing drawing-room.
'Isn't it most unkind,' Lady Nora commented, 'how your
GAA has thrown a smokescreen over everything you yearn
To expose? You can't name the names, poor fellow.'

I've been thinking of my mother's life, the sheer audacity
Of her kindness, of her unbridled largesse. She who had

Nothing or little to give gave more than the shirt off her back,
Gave the skin of her hands to break wet firewood in a hard frost
During the long winter of 1962–63. The long winter settled

Across her shoulders as an oxen-yoke of pain. The hard facts
Of Irish life distilled what was left of my mother's lost poetry;

Blackbirds pitied her in her Council terrace, came for crumbs
That would give them stomach pains of frost. The proud

Of soul were betrothed to her alone, an old soldier
Escaped from the Lismore Union, Johnny Dubliner down

On his luck in a ditch between Dromana Wood and Cappoquin,
Pitiable Seventh Day Adventists who stayed for tea and

Offered her watchwords of literacy. The sky of Ireland,
That bitter, grey, unforgiving Blackwater sky, that bitter

Wind, that wind of snobbery and *schadenfreude*, that bitter
Chill of the bitter with their double stitches of bitterness,

With their little shit of bitterness, with their shit that fell
Upon the frozen paths where she laid the only warm straw

She owned, the only straw laid beneath the Cappoquin shoeless;
That bitter little winter called life knew nothing of her planitude.

I can't say that the day smiled on us, or that anything smiled,
As we dared the wet earth in our wet digging clothes.
The late Mrs Cockburn was in no mood to chat. It was she,
After all, who was being evicted by a cruel remote-control:
A letter sent from Toronto that saw the summer spoilt.
She had just published a good book, her autobiography
That kept her friends straight and her enemies crooked,
But as if the world needed to show a woman of quality
What indifference meant, or how landlords could still be shit,
The letter was not an offer for film rights but a notice to quit.

We approached the bed of agapanthus in a deathly quiet.
What I thought was *umbellatus* and a big mistake
For the small place where she was headed was, as a matter
Of fact and not any other kind of insufferable organic fact,
A huge clump of the smaller *orientalis*, sometimes called
Agapanthus *mooreanus*, and perfect, as I should have
Known. I knew that Mrs Consuela White was up in Lismore
And would soon be on the phone to me. Mrs Cockburn
Also knew that, though they were old friends, Mrs White's chilling
Remarks, her wicked *schadenfreude*, could kill African lilies.

IN A FRUIT CAGE

It's astonishing the way a passage of time has worked upon
This one last raspberry. The late surveyor-wasps of autumn, like me,

Test and measure with their thousand eyes the flesh
Of late aromatic fruit, this one red world of perishable

Goods, subjected now to a cool, fastidious measurement
Of insects, insects urgent with signals of survival –

In contrast to me, I must admit; myself less troubled
By what this globe of fleshly red contains; this wound

Of colour that stains us both inside my fruit cage. The
Hours, it seems, turn more slowly inside my own life, and

Fruit seems not a food at all, but something from art,
A bleeding metaphor, perhaps, of those fears and desires;

Of all the efforts of human will that insects lack, all the
Stained reticence of things that must, yet again, be cut back.

I am still climbing. We are not going back
To the damp basement where there was a princess
In a golden frame, her Formica coming unstuck.
I am still climbing to the sunlit attic room
Where The Clash are playing. It is 'Lon-
don Calling' that I hear from the asbestos stairs.
While Gregory O'Donoghue and Paddy Galvin
Lived here, there was still a lot of fun in England.

Now the heart has gone from Camden town
Though its music survives as I walk inland,
Not the Glanmire Station or Grantham goods –
It is the hollow Tube ping a solid
Les Paul, fretful whine of a London train,
That particular tone as if Philip Larkin
Had formed a Brynmor Jones Band;
The bass gone haywire, but the lead still grand.

Here is an absence peopled with references from books.
This chapel's bank account has been frozen, this boy
Beside me has a garment with bitterness for a mother;
And a troubled face of mother-of-pearl. His looks
Are those of a lost shepherd. He claims no other
Place but here in this monstrosity without joy,
This strangely beautiful; this one Jerusalem:
Home is a flock lost at night, or a hypothetical Rome,

Or something in the silence of a steel engraving
From your old books. I'm thinking of that long view
Of the city from the road to Bethany, the star-
Shaped walls under cloud, sunlight tinting
The cumulus with silver and white. From afar
There's the lost cantor's son, a yellow glaze of Israel
Upon the stained earth. *Shush!* The coffee cup, the kiss
Of light, falls on the Rabbi you have loved for years

And somebody begins to play the Fantasia of Bach's
Partita in A Minor – suddenly a torrent of light
Falls upon us all, an improvised device of music
To lift immemorial squalor, to ease heartache
And dispossession; to let us not perish
In the bitter pandemonium of those who fall in
With God. We rest against a most wretched, ancient wall
And kiss again where notes and pelargonia blossoms fall.

And the young spill from the upturned casket of
A sublime Vesuvius: night adjusts its golden coif.
A strand or two of blond is wayward
On this evening's red carpet, light is poured
From anxious tapers, a breeze blows off the desert;
This night is restored to where the sea may start
Again, given a moon's encouragement;
Given the calmed El Nino, the calm heaven-sent

In the Santa Ana hills, pellucid as Orvieto
In Virgil's wine glass, homely as bundled calico
From the farthest markets of the new empire.
These are the arranged hours, streaked with desire,
That General Electric captures in its holy grid,
Hours to invite Bogart in, or dismiss Ovid,
With a wave from the young director's chair.
The red carpet spreads from Pershing Square

And finds a frayed end in the darkened sand.
In the sandstone malls, in markets underground,
Food vendors bellow from the far reaches of the north,
Opals tug at the purse strings of the heart,
Books on low tables speak to you of eternal youth;
In pine barrows are DVDs of the entire planet.
Here is a stall that pretends you need water, here
Is spring in a cold bottle. A Goth wipes the windows clear.

It must have been like this in the best homes of Pompeii.
Barola hours decanted from glazed vessels, a fine day

Dissolving into another fine day. There was a foolish
Notion that dress was informal, the young could wish
For a loincloth, the old for a toga –
Except this: beauty is formalised in limb and patina,
A gift, only, of the exceptional and the rich;
Here the old turn to ash before they soil the beach.

World-famous through its reproduction, Venice is
The original of itself: unreal, shunning oil for water.
Only a Doge could turn his back on the Veneto,
Resplendent in trade, clothed in a satin seawater;
Perpetually liquid as a merchantman of Murano glass.
Ah, it is ever the genius of love-making and putting on
Clothes, a neoclassical *Don't look now*, or a cold,
Melancholic gazer-upon blond boys as in
Thomas Mann's *Der Tod in Venedig*. Here is a Lord
On a pilgrimage of sorts, captured in water,
His countess in the canal, drowning. St Marks is wet
With a determined and deflected Brenta. The sea
Is only a layer of fixative upon a Venetian canvas:
Gondoliers remain frantic in the workshop of Titian,
Touching up the edges with poles, 'a-oel!' *Only water*.

Nothing holds you back from the road like a song,
A song that seems so long, a phrase like a night light
That gives us a key and a poem and another
Song just for good behaviour; the song
That is as slow and deliberate and porcelain
As the three swans we saw ambling along
The quays at lighthouse level, three
Children of Lir just transformed into
Flight, their wings moving without comment,
Their very purposefulness as beautiful
As the folklore that turns unselfconsciously here
In a lamplit public house on the Aran Islands
When all the candles have burned out –
The ones left over from the Christmas crib;
And the little silver menorah you brought
All the way from a Haifa market
When you were just out of a Waterford
Convent school and as innocent as a swan
In the evening, a green drop of Irish girl
Like a pot of moisturiser in the sun-baked
Kibbutz before the whole wide world
Went to the dogs; the dog of war, the dog
That has now made a scholarly girl's
Simple efforts to make the desert bloom
Seem like the most appalling betrayal:
Yet it is hardly foolish to have loved a Jewish
Boy, even if he took away the only photo
Of you when you were as beautiful as
A tall willow in the rain, as an olive tree in the sun.

Late April dresses the house in a kinder light. Today is green
And green covers the insomnia of stones and the pallor of ogham.

Bear with us, April, as we turn from the sickening years.
The unbuttoned white hedgerows are not glass but tears,

The trees have been handled roughly and shaken to pieces,
Even the crows are bleeding. Here, fog lifts and releases

Apologetic light – darting cursors of small birds,
Emphysemic cows. The sky holds nothing fluid or untoward,

Nothing but the formal turn of the day;
A weak light falling on rutted wheat fields and clay,

And fresh leaves turning like small finches in the breeze,
Birds anchored at the node, full of the necessities

Of birdlife and sickened by the thought of trees.
I button your dress by the window, kiss your bare knees

With all the abandon of the penniless. Come, let us
Walk back to the year when we last borrowed money, let us

Ease our quantitative selves: the bird that stole my pay cheque
Has left the land in winter clothes, is never coming back.

You walk the between-world of the seashore,
neither seal nor dog but metamorphosis.
This is where the universe dropped us. Let's
get used to it. At least we have water:
the great gold-hoard of the blue planet,
water that creates its seasonal drama,
its timely ebb and flow, its lunar infiltrations.

Here comes a coastal express of time that skirts
the seashore between dogs and seals. It –
I mean time – it is more than water.
In its passage it dislodges oceans.
Time, rather than water, pulls up at this platform
in Oceanside, California, more than thirty years ago;
though, for time, it is now; and more than water.

Your feet sink deeply into the cadmium wash of sand,
Leaving toes spattered with burnt umber, with zinc
White and ivory black of miniature pebbles. You rise
With toes full of the sea's handiwork, with spatters
Of cerulean blue; with bristles of flame red:
Nothing the sea does is overworked. Even gold leaf is
Stippled and removed. Upon cold toes you walk back,
Scrambling between rocks left polished by the ebb tide –

Like going back to the studio after twenty years away;
Not with new colours, for colour is the thing least needed,
But with a set of sharp blades, each blade as fine as the edge
Of a nerve; each blade sharpened by the sea to cut away colour,
Each blade tempered for its own colour: the colour of sadness,
The colour of history, the colour of departure, of jealousy,
Of everything that being in the world throws into water:
The canvas, when you finish, becoming a reflex of waves.

THE LATE WIND

The late wind again is like a disturbed aunt
Who rattles the doorbell of a door gone missing.

The heart of the month has lost its hatpin,
It returns too soon in a panic of threads –

Even the windows tremble with fever
As I toss and turn in the moist eiderdown.

We have been in bed for five long months,
Ever since the weather turned bad

In this part of the world. I doubt we will ever
Rise again unless one of our mothers

Comes back to life. If you smell something
Going on in the kitchen please tell us,

For this disturbed wind has pierced
Our souls. A south-westerly has wounded us.

Only the smell of lamb stew from another era
Could make us stand against the wind:

No friend standing upright, provident and unhinged,
No door but a mother knocking in the wind.

I am sorry for the night sky
that has had to share
my own gloomy wakefulness.
For it is not the star's fault

or any fault of immaculate heaven
that an event occurred, a star burned,
in the childhood of my soul.
The universe has been much more

than a good-enough mother,
giving me time as an eternal playpen
and a wondrous cloud of blue.
I can see the stars shine upon me

with their mirror neurons. They are
mindful of my toes growing cold
but cannot move an arm. This duvet
slips like a careless caretaker.

Night is free of the chemical of fear
but my toes are wakeful still –
Where a star sheered away
from its mother, the night is blue.

The sea recedes yet again with its fabulous ingratitude. It leaves the mark of its eating on the least sand; a detritus of shell, shrimp abandoned in goblets of stone, a napkin trail of shredded kelp and weed. The sea left early while we struggled with the stove. Late rain fell on embers that promised to have us fed, though you, goddess of poetry, you drove the wind a little our way, creasing the fire with red and sending blue smoke against the sea. We may never get back to the more organic rhythms before the wild part began. We are as witless as spindly sandpipers dancing on the keyboard of the tides. Did the sea have a good time while we hammered and traded on the shore? Even dolphins swam inland at the port of Cork to see what we were partying for. They have erred on the side of caution.

Waves thump these old red sandstone cliffs and retreat with shattered nerves. There is little evidence left behind, save water and iodine at the scene of the crime, a sea far out like the century coming back to haunt us. Don't speak a word of drownings in this surge of time: it is wrack floating. I peer over the tall cliff at this body of a boy lately washed ashore, body of a murdered one who came from afar. It seems that we've become the last field for the sorrows of the world. Layer upon layer, bogland above the sea, corners of the sea-field where the sun lies down in the west to die: it seems that the world wishes to present us with a great gift of unhappiness, a little something to gild our sea. A gull parachutes where the gannets dive. Every explosion will make them blind. What if Ezra Pound had fought in the Resistance like these sea-birds? What if, instead of mouthing insanities, he had scurried at night with false passports for downed fighters or delivered die-stamps and phials of ink to Père Benoît. Europe. What if, it asks me, what if he'd done something noble instead, would you read those words differently, those purple marks: 'silk', 'phalloi', 'lily-of-the-valley'?

Even this perished red stone, pear-shaped and powdery as it dries in my hand, even this igneous rock has striations of memory. These white streaks, for all the world like ice-cream in an old ice-wafer, tell of some crystallised trauma, some abusive event in the biography of stone. I place it carefully here where salt water meets the shore, at the lowest point of the tide. I expect, like the long, unbroken trail of the damaged, that it will seek comfort in something bigger than itself: so that the sea with its regular coming and going must seem at times – to a perished rock – like the act of listening, like a counselling of ages. I think water is hoarding its best ideas as it settles in this hidden rock pool. Depths become stagnant as they thicken with sand. Fronds of dislodged sea wrack, a hermit crab searching for an upgrade, vacated rooms of mussel shells, all pass through the mind of water. Only the wider tide, I believe, could change both our minds. Even now, rock-flounders wish they could become heroic – waiting here in this rock pool for the flash of flesh, homeless crab or lugworm: hidden in sand, their mouths wide open to please the night-editor, the sea. Some mollusc will lose decorum. I throw them a by-line with bait attached. And wait. Only when the tide turns shall we have the news.

This water has been a torturer since early daybreak, since impatient dawn – before we rose – announced its programme. I fear these rocks may be fooled into thinking they're drowning as waves ebb and flow, ebb and flow – though it is history that calls the sea back before rocks reveal their sources, history that hoards its agents: periwinkle, cockles and mussels. Such terrors! Here, the sea remains calm while it tells us of unpleasant things. My bare feet are in the sea and a froth of salt and water washes over me the way time does in its own ebb and flow. It is power and its relentless wave motion that hits the sand. What has gone out will come back again, sure as the moon. If I lower myself and become wet all over I can hear the applause of that November in the not-too-long-ago. In this Kerry surf it is the crowd around Dick Spring, kingmaker, a Labour wave called *1992*; a cleansing wash around my ankles; time's wry promises. Look, the sun rising, the half-empty coffee cup, the spent cigar. It is John Coltrane and Miles Davis (folks, listen!), all trumpet and tenor saxophone. Impatient is such music of the sea, tide and outcrop of songs, caves and currents and such dangerous kinds of darkness. Now, beyond our island the sea is on fire, waves make a successful landing, leaving behind, it must be said, shadowy urchins, molluscs to piss upon. Ah, time to bathe the blackbird.

We marvel at the phosphorescence of stars between clouds – that very particular stage design, those walk-on clouds, the monstrous ego of the heavens. Night doesn't hang around for the applause but you move to the edge of the balcony. You straighten the sky with a gesture of respect: you utter a Christian prayer, no less. The house has become an awkward paperback, too wet with pungent sky. With me it is not so much the Milky Way as the Cointreau and cream, the last cocktail shaker in the clouds. These nights, the universe may be at its best when it's spinning. In a milky centrifuge I pick up signals; news from the farthest away places, galaxies that mirror grief because we look upon them. Now stars are drowned in a cascade of rage. So many shredded wafers of water; the wind sings suddenly of heartbreak and passion, obscuring stars, sending us indoors: summer drives home its thesis in ochre streams. See the winds blow in an arranged sequence of fatal flow charts. You wouldn't believe the marked cards, dripping wet, that blow along this canyon of unrest. In sagging wires wind whines like the dismal, untidy death. The hour is stripped to the bone, so it is, and banks grown bare that were verdant and fulsome. Autumn rainfall skips from channel to channel, seeking the quickest way to escape; the damp leaf, the bare branch, the unforgiving element –

It is not so much the smell of the sea as the tide's sucking after-breath. The sky is iodine where we lie and, though the wind can never tell the truth so close to the ocean, the facts of the day fall on wet sand. Here is the wrack of the hour, here the sun-baked wreckage. Here, I have Agustín Lara for company. I do think of him as I listen, and through him all of sad Mexico singing its very first bolero. We are all together by the sea in these Bakelite tides. The wind is driving hard but the piano comes in waves, bobbing between the heavy velvet curtains of the swell. Here comes your lost love, a tragic Lupita Palomera, still singing with a swimmer's broken heart. Sing to us of heavy tropical rains, shelter in our lives, our frail pavilions – breathe in again, for it's never difficult to praise what rises from the sea. Even oystercatchers never attempt your singular, long epic of pain, but sprint instead towards the single line, the shingle, the unsuspecting worm. Ebbing and flowing like pilot-fish on legs, they rise with the hope of things and halt, for a split second, before the sea throws the book at them or offers a higher grade. Being a bird is perpetual learning, but never melancholy. What they know is that knowledge comes upturned, in bitter songs, in wet coquettish offerings.

This late wind, you'd never guess,
Is hardly our scholarly business,
Though the trees make it theirs,
Quite reasonably, and the air
Of heaven dislodges more than fruit.
No storm blew the candle out
Where the trees are, but human heat
That blew up not down. In truth,
Human commerce made the trees
Weep in the wind. As Tarquinius
Wept in his sibylline distress
When nine trees of knowledge fell
Upon the false promises of a Sybil.

A sudden squall makes me look up:
Mid morning and this blazing hawthorn
Has reached its heady eigentone;
The impious vibrations of trees
Comes to grief in a guitar of leaves;

Clouds' lentical excretes a sun
As severe and purple as a new pope
Who threatens fruit with novation.
Such fear has entered the lapsed trees
They shed vestments now, they weep.

Though this harbour may carry things across,
It simply cannot hypothesise
The way a blue Dutch dredger does.
The harbour is all eyes of small craft
In sunlight: such squinting of a pilot boat
As it creates a long white squiggle. The hour
Is wet beneath its cradle, but time is bone
Dry on Haughey's timbers of the harbour.
I fry these non-commissioned eggs
On a buckled shovel; I make tea from the sea.

The tent's fly-sheet begins to speak,
a story as old as Homer
from the Blasket Islands. *Rain!*
An unearthly squall and huge drops
typing furiously on our canvas,
guy lines straining, spattered corrections,
wind offering advice in every direction.
Here, a squall of pencils at dawn
drenches the whole library with colour;
long editions of vermilion fuchsia, volumes
of flattened browns and ochres.
A few drops have penetrated this
groundsheet, to demand more, as I turn
in my small polyester boat, known
As a boy again, applying Tippex to rain.

Our kitten turns to deliver its encomium,
Purring as if a lump of tabby quartz
Propelled it so. It shares this petrichor
With the last bumblebees seeking glamour.
Wet stones release their chatoyant gaze
As I shake Molly's cocktail shaker.
Here is quartered lime after unexpected rain:
We have lost our house, but earth is warm
Beneath your cherished tintinnabulation.

A beech leaf falls precisely on this narrow emptied space
Left by a fountain pen. It's not that there was a storm,
Or any hint of a storm, in this painfully private Sunday.
Colour supplements and unsold houses flooded in upon
The *ennui* at the end of our era. It was bad while it lasted.

The sun came out and went in again, the lottery was played
And so many marked cards that might have been significant
Accumulated like these well-spent leaves in a beech grove.
A little Celtic blackbird taps at the window, wanting to be
Let into the reflected image of itself. In its reflexive room

A bird could stitch through old embroidery with ease –
Time to pull away, the leaf must have thought, *time*
To arrest the osmosis. If it is poison that Ireland
Is best at then time to risk chlorophyll. This event has drawn a line
Across the written page, a beech is the last to show its hand.

A satin veil displaces cold air
In October's susurrant hour.
It is not flesh, but wings
That engulf the frosted glass.
A barn owl's diaphanous
Hunt begins above my head –

Midnight's nebulous labourer,
Night's cherished daughter,
Luxuriates above me: a confetti
Of rats and mice, a heavenly
Moon; all scatter for the bride.

Such stories brought home by the foraging honeybee: the world
Is too corporate now, the nitrogen-rich call centre has growth
Fatigue, greenish scum covers the breath in hayfield and stream.
Listen now, the stars are beginning to tell us their stories too.
The very far stars, that is; signals picked up, no doubt,
By the faltering beehives in Ned Lonergan's farm. Only this
Very morning we were astonished to hear of the vacant hive,
The second one, where the bees had left without giving notice,

The hive, now, become a little apartment block of cells for rent.
I thought of the clever ones in the European Space Centre
And how they've just picked up a new celestial music,
A signal with a watery cadence from a distant sister Earth.
Twenty light years from Hennessy's farm a beehive
In a planet that is dedicated to peace has just received
Its exhausted colonists: bees that heard, long before physics,
Of fields far away, dandelions, clean rivers, white Dutch clover.

GRUNEWALD

in memory of Brian Lenihan T. D.

The sea is a wet preacher at Passiontide.
This Europe is a nest of Expressionists

From which, at any moment, a God
May rise to dry His dark wings.

The Euro may increase but we will decrease.
Here, on this rock, a lamb.

Waves rise with the helpless efforts
Of an Irish taxpayer. Cormorants carry you.

I can see the wreckage of us far out at sea;
Our wreckage receding still. The pilot boat,

With all its unused life-belts,
Has a black stain on the prow where you

Were pushed, Brian. Black gulls return
To their roosting grounds, Brussels, Berlin.

Not the Brahminy Kite, then, that robs squawking crows
And common creatures of their food; not that friend
Of Vishnu hunting the wide waters of Mumbai,
But the common Pariah Kite that Shakespeare
Knew and named for a friend of Autolycus.
Now, I see its quills banded with dark crossbars,
White beneath its beak, rufous at the tail,

All in light and buoyant flight. It is a friend
Of boys and, like them, a scavenger of small worlds.

Its mewing squeal as it circles the rigging of our boat
Seems like the humble afterglow of a good play:
Its gossip is an unconsidered trifle. Its traffic is sheets.

I stand with Zhao Lihong under a street lamp
In the leafy French Concession. We are waiting for Ai Qing
Who has gone home to teach history in the meadows.
Once it was the boat to Chong Ming, now it's a bridge;
Once it was terrible to be condemned, but now
We have this comforting light from the street lamp

That Zhao Lihong made. The incandescent light
Must seem old-fashioned now, shedding its warm glow
On our aging forms, but also upon the very young.
Plate glass and concrete may be insanely bright,
But is it deep? Is it deep as the riverbed of the Yellow
River? Will anything be as deep as the crown

Of the osmanthus tree, flowering a thousand years,
As Robert Bly promised us, or Zhao Lihong
In his greatest poem? Zhao's street lamp lights
A crowded street, Shanghai so beautiful it draws tears,
A soldier politely coughing when I get a name wrong,
Applause from the rain when my address is right –

And then the red azalea of someone lighting a match:
Cigarette smoke brings Ai Qing to me. It is he
From the long-ago when I was very young:
His poetry like cigarette smoke. No poetry-patch
Will protect us from the urge to make poems –
I am going home to Chong Ming with Zhao Lihong.

We marvel at the stars in a clear October night.
My companion marvels at galaxies beyond sight.
There are millions of them in the known unknown.
That star may be dead from where light was emitted,

My friend explains. It may be dead a million years.
Darkened into truth, I reply 'So what –
Isn't it we who give the stars meaning?
We dream and write poems, making the stars great.'

The look of disappointment on his young Chinese face
Is as dark as the greatest infinity of space.
He is disappointed in me on behalf of the night sky,
But now I'm on a roll, warped by Irish whiskey,

And I won't let infinity lie. When he speaks of probes
Sent to the unknown, I say it's the space between the earlobes
Of Donald Rumsfeld that needs exploring, and quick;
For the sake of all humankind, as well as Philip K. Dick.

STARLINGS OVER TERMINI STATION

for Maurice Harmon's eightieth birthday

Starlings like poets have no concept of the wide world,
Not for them what is orchestral or a greater master plan,
But as they wheel and bank over Termini Station,
As they lift in a brownish cloud in the winter cold,

They keep an eye on only seven companions in the sky.
So it is with poets, I think. Poets have seven companions
In a long or short life; one who collects the first medallions,
One who soon follows with a sharp unerring eye

And earns the praise of strangers, one who will fall
Early in an Antarctic of alcohol, his phrases covered with snow,
One who will marry well, travel and never want to know
A thing about poets *ever, ever* again; one who hears the call

To Catholic priesthood, one who emigrates to teach textual
Analysis, who grows angrier every day with books from home,
And one who knows that an Italian physicist, electric monitors on,
Keeps watching rooftops where sparrows bank and wheel.

AT NEWCASTLE CENTRAL

for Theo Dorgan

This train glides in through a cross-hatch of stars,
A brief respite down England's throbbing spine
This early summer's night; a casting-off
Of Mayflies taken away by the Trans-Pennine
To feed to praying mothers along the banks of the Wear.
We halt where Basil Bunting was much made of,

But not before looking back, in the vain hope
That a librarian from Hull might have disembarked
With a Sidney Bechet LP. You want to get ahead
To our berth under Earl Grey, but I hesitate, still,
For I am sure I saw the ghost of Osbert Sitwell,
Escaped from Scarborough, now bowing his head

At my copy of *Before the Bombardment*
Bought for a song in the station bookstall at Tynemouth –
But it is a portly gentleman, not unlike Osbert Sitwell
In later years, and a host of Incarnate Sitwells who breathe
Their Renishaw songs over our unhappy Irish baggage,
Like *monsignori* blessing babies in far Montegufoni.

SLOW FOOD

I would like to feed this child who is dying with slow food,
So that time might stand still for him, so that a grandfather
Clock might not fall apart in his arms. All of the laziness of air

In our warm temperate climate, all the anxious hands
Of young barristers at this morning's Farmers' Market,
All of this complete snobbery of the gut, might bear down

Upon one dying child. Here is my Euro, child. Here is
The olive oil and the stuffed artichoke. Here is the conscience
And the conscience money. They stole my land too,

They took my small cottage apart, stone by stone.
They surveyed all of us and we nearly died. I am sending, child,
Very fast Irish food from my evicted great grandmother.

You spent your entire life as if you'd come to an arrangement.

There were no precise notes about life in your Hermes *Béarn* wallet,
Though we found your last twelve poems, flowery and indecent,
In a folder of bright red Tadelakt calfskin. This is the interim set,

The note attached said, *death is not a full stop, but a silver*

and palladium tab. You spent an entire season in precious metal
while the rest of us ran around town with base numbers.
You heated your metal one phrase at a time, sealing

All the work in leather only. You avoided scrap dealers

And the egregious second-rate: it was not light but heat,
It was not beer but well-racked wine. A woman in furs
And her nine elegant boys, a chauffeur who liked whiskey neat –

You were carried by such carriers of apricot and amber.

Now the art dealers are crowding your marble foyer. There is a crop
Of crushed dandelions all over your Afghan kilim; and you've escaped
Behind the silver H-stop where you are rolled in a teak cigar, though still
In a state of undress. What to wear! Dead poet, it must be a nightmare.

John F. Deane, *Eye of the Hair* (Carcanet, £9.95)
John Goodby, *A True Prize* (Cinnamon, £7.95)
Peter McDonald, *Torchlight* (Carcanet, £9.95)

Here are three books on the warm Ballyferriter sand.
I am wiping grains from Deane's *Eye of the Hare*
As I read again his prize-winning words, 'Our island
Shoemaker' and 'or bread, or music, what I am stitching for

Is Christ'. The very words that won the Greg O'Donoghue
Prize in memory of Cork's much-loved poet,
Are words this Achill Christian always found true –
From seminary to late middle-age, whole worlds rotate

Around Deane's fundamental Catholic training.
This new book is a Deaney reclamation
Once more: God in cedar, in exhaled breathing,
Presentation parlours of Mary Leland or K. O'Brien;

All fold together in 'Chewing on Stones'
Or 'Mayo Theology' with 'Bible pages open
To show the history of God.' Such poems
Brave Satan, such poems are a hymn

And summation of Deane's lifelong search
For God in books, for Rome in lamplit homes.
Tea spills on 'Weeds and Wilderness' as I lurch
Forward into a canvas shelter. A squall drones

Off Brandon as I read of 'fern-world
In a usual fox-den stink and darkness'
And marvel at Deane's capacity to enfold
Both God and eight-hand reels in poetic dress:

For that's his gift, this difficult poet –
Cranky with God, troubled with hares,
He ties hope and patience in a knot
To offer insight, to catch us unawares.

*

Many will remember John Goodby at UCC,
A neat disciple of Modernism, a free
Verbal blackguard lost to Swansea.
He writes of Welsh Christmas and Uzbeki,

Of Ballycotton and Blenheim Square,
With the aplomb of a man in a cage.
Glottal stops and isophonics, despair
At RP, this fellow never fails to engage

At every level of anxiety.
From Corkery's Gardiner's Hill
To a slowly oscillating crank
And Dafydd ap Gwilym's penis,

Not to mention 'The Light Inside',
A great, ventilating sequence
Of outpatients, cashpoints, fire screens
And suiter-withering aunts.

Goodby is today's Dylan Thomas,
Welsh as can be but hesitant, puritan
In a youthful way, tuning up the West
In the East; a new poet of the *Odeon*.

*

First poem in McDonald's *Torchlight*
Is familiar from the pages of the *TLS*:
A poem about crying through the night
With half the Group Theatre upstairs

And going like babies after a performance
In Mary O'Malley's Belfast days.
This poem is as perfect as any arranged
On any page. It is one of the ways

Poetry stays alive: to recall the dead
Or the gone, or the going, with such love
That a mother comes back to the poet's bed
To mother anxious actors before they move.

Sharp, Classical too, and minimal,
McDonald creates a new Hymn to Demeter,
Though Persephone's implacable
Grudge against *Eire* still holds water

Through all kinds of Belfast childhoods.
It is the sweet seed of pomegranate
That this good poet chews upon, for food
And text. His translation is first-rate

And lengthy, formal and true –
As is the bitter fragment of Sappho
With poor Tithonus getting his due;
A destiny as precipitous as the Euro.

McDonald's range is wide,
From Sapphic odes to 'The Orange ABC',
Blue skies above the Loyalist countryside
Hitching rides from the kindly RUC

And such moments in the alternative
Myth to our own dear Emerald Isle.
Highly educated, he has poetic nerve;
And, like Rory McIlroy, he has Ulster style.

Who should have known better, being the son
Of a Latin adverb, spent his every waking hour
In forms of attack upon O'Connell and Moore:
His hatred of them went beyond the bounds of reason
Into the realm of translating both. Clongownians
And those schooled by Jesuit Royalists at St Acheul
Were perplexed by his satires, but never asked why
A priest of such learning gave his life to small rhymes –

All a matter, surely, of fame; jealousy and its attendant despair:
How we are always sure that others suffer less for the palm
Than we have suffered. Fluent in French and Latin,
Demented with difficult rhymes, he heard St Peters'
Bells as Shandon chimes, such Classical bells as make plain
That each poet has to run his very own marathon.

I'm calling in all the cats on a bad night for black kittens.
As I get older in this land of Ireland I'm calling more

Simple creatures home, even if it isn't a winter's night,
In a country driven insane by too much rainwater.

I'll be housing all the infirm and four-legged friends –
Two by two they'll meow past the opened door,

Not knowing what night's abroad. Yeats and his friends,
And other hosts of darkness, come bearing torches.

I wish I was far away. In Macalester, for example,
Set in its reasonable snow, where ceremony happens

But only as a metaphor, trick-or-treat, or snap-apple.
All the cats of Minnesota file neatly through the door.

The world, that time, had a flower-strewn base
And every poem seemed to fit the anthemia panel
That God in his wisdom had chosen to place
Above the gadrooned acanthus, feet scrolled

And canted, and glittering of ormolu
In the fire that burned beneath Lady Inez.
The Brigadier and I were happy to have come through,
Though I was happier than he – amazed, even –

To have escaped the searing flames of the poor.
I was no fool. I knew even as a boy with a load
Of timber from Glenshelane Wood that to be sure
Of Heaven was the height of foolishness. Untold

Deaths had scarred my old companion – war
And history, Eton, the Guards. Only the BBC
At the cenotaph could force his aged tears.
Remembrance was the nearest he could get to poetry

While I was drenched in its pollen like a child
Who had upturned a bowl of lilies. *Lilium*
Leaned across my path: it lay unspoiled
For weeks while I made up my own spoilt mind –

Whether to make a poem of its passing or to forget.
Words had all the time in the world. A white marble
Pedestal felt light in my hands; a Dolmen's weight
Had been lifted from my shoulders. All went well.

AN AIRPORT FOR EGRETS

It must seem like so much unnecessary haste
To deliberate egrets who thought it no waste

To wait a millennium, even two, to reach
This island from a subtropical beach,

So much propulsive haste, to fly back and forth
For one fortnight at a time. I am stuck at this airport,

Like a wingless bird in a colony of sloth.
Labels flap like bog cotton in the undergrowth;

The wind in this atrium blows an Atlantic gale,
Travellers like egrets are growing porcelain-pale

While the luggage consoles shimmer and flash
In a roosting struggle with new volcanic ash.

Birds seem to say we should wait a thousand years
To travel so far, or wait till a millennium clears

The ash from this human need to make a hotel
Of the whole world: every frail egret could tell

The time to fly by the heat of the vineyard:
Not the sun-worshipper, but the sun-timed bird.

Fallen martyrs of Antioch, time's unrecoverable flora –
It's not me, it's the garden itself that becomes nostalgic
At this time of year. There's a chill in the steel engraving
Of September and that arch opportunist, Piranesi,
Moves from the fallen triumph of spent roses,
Withered fruit canes, berries that have given up on God,
To set his easel where the view might be sold, yet again,
In a grey tourism of compost. Spring is now as distant
As the star anemone, or potentilla *quinquefolia*;
Or the ovate, aromatic white flower of strawberry
That seemed as fresh as a young Centurion in the heat
Of last May. As for the primitive rose so loved by Pliny
And its two hundred varieties that filled the Coliseum,
There's nought but an odorous aftertaste. There is
Nothing to be done as the page turns, the two of us forking
Old potato stalks, the year shriven before pagan idols.

A UNIONIST INTELLECTUAL OF THE TWENTIES

in memory of W. E. D. Allen

This is the seedy place, Connolly Station, seats as red
As a brothel and as plastic as a disease. In a railway café,
Their one lost Republic, brutish as Fassbinder's *Lola*
Or the Hamburg whorehouse in *Smiley's People*.
They have lost all discipline to keep despair in check
As if another Catholic martyr had died here,
Ballad-singing, with the grace of sausages and ketchup.
I need to be where life has meaning, my own Belfast
And Portadown, the regal comfort of Antrim,
Tidiness of Ulster breasts as our flappers move
In such boyish linen. I shift on this disgruntled Dublin seat.

        True, it is a long way from *Unionist* West Belfast
To poorly designed billboards of the new Soviet in Tbilisi.
I kept my head down, I grew a shaggy beard,
I sheltered behind a carved wooden door
While Turk and Persian fought six long wars
In the Ponto-Caspian isthmus; intrigues in Kartli
And Kakheti, Byzantine missions in Ossetia,
And I noted, yet again, the historic ineptitude
Of all southern princes: all the while, be quiet behind a door,
Is what Ulster taught me – this ebb and flow,
This flare-up and Catholic intrigue, this way with icons.

        All of which brings me to that point about Belfast
Printing, about the matter of theatre posters in 1857 –
What might have been printed came just too late.

It is the way with history. A change of khan provokes
A crisis: the fort at Sunzha, the link at Astrakhan,
First Russian contacts with the Georgian kings,
Empires stuck on mountains while England went maritime –
So that, as I descended the Asiatic snowline
In a limousine of the Abkhazian OGPU, so far from Ulster,
Turning into Leninski Prospekt, past wounded *vaziri*,
It was bad printing made me angry. It was lowercase.

I am leaving this vineyard to hang out with Jeremiah.
Anyway, the first pick of the grapes is almost in. *Anyway*,
There are enough people to finish this old job. Let
The creels overflow without me. I am going west
Across the Shannon where the last Jeremiah lives.
I hear the catcalls of his miserable companions, I smell
The wet turf that can never be brought in: nothing less
Than Jeremiah, and all his turf-cutting children,
Have been calling me back home. *Anyway*, it's from whence
I came one dark day after the hydrogen bomb.
All the roads to Zion are in mourning; Jerusalem
Has sinned, and filth clings to all our clothes. *Anyway*.

BEL CANTO

for Catherine Coakley

The year has been detained because of something offstage,
Some disturbance in the wings that had drawn the Stage Manager
And all his gruff attendants into a minor skirmish –
What might have seemed to the innocent as a skittish wind
Making the curtains flutter was in fact a delicate elbow
And a Greek or Cypriot raised knee coming to blows. The Irish
Need to remain in their seats, was what Ms Legarde said
As she came front-stage, checking her Louis Vuitton buttons,
Adjusting her coiffure. At least we were sitting here, my father
Said, so we can't be blamed for this wounded orchestra.
O *patria! Dolce, e ingrate patria*, the young Latvian beauty
Sang with a restrained sweetness. Violins assembled
Doubtfully around her, but they all tried honestly to come in.
It was Europe trying to adjust itself, but more simply now:
It was Christine Lagarde and Elina Garanca together,
Making all the violins murmur, just murmur. There now,
My father whispered, that's it: *Tancredi*, Act 1, the *Andante*.

Admit it: in the end we are all Catalan.
This one idea of Europe is dead:
Daniel Cohn-Bendit speaks for himself.

In the cave of ourselves his voice is hollow,

Leaving a sincere French mark upon stone.
We will ever go round and round
Like Saltee seabirds seeking a haven –

Out of our mist, it is always famine ships,

Forebears, archipelagos. The wreck of our ship
Is the birth of economies. A rock pierces hide,
An outhouse is filled to the stars.

Our cattle grid has devoured treasuries.

Give us no more of the well-bred child, Europe's
Sole survivor. An armada of protocols
Has shed its load off our coast. Heaven-sent,

A squall of blue stars has swallowed Europe.

This garden is full of holes where I've been digging like a dog;
Fruit trees are lopped sideways in the earth's inlaid tabletop.
Ghosts everywhere in the worm-like white of nettle roots:
I disentangle them from the spaghetti of gooseberry root-balls:
Working this late in the year and full of a hopeless guilt.
Mrs Bowen, someone has stolen our medallion, that's what
I feel like saying as I stumble between the two discontented
Half-spaniels, dripping wet with the early sleet. This garden,
Also, has gone to the dogs. It is a good picture of many parts

Of the year, wretched and overstretched. But here I begin again,
God help us, like every hopeless gardener, for I see the light
Of another season just over the hill of Christmas. My own face
In a pool of mud, my hands grey and brown like the hands
Of ghosts trapped in the sleety veil of December. The house
On a hill, its windows yellow with light, colour of whiskey
And full of the whiskey's heat. I need a flask right here,
As the dead do, needing to come with us towards a season
Instead of their home in earth; cabins without moon-phases.
I can feel the dead who gardened just behind my left shoulder,
Breathing fretfully upon me, like Milton upon Robert Graves.
Not the Anglo-Irish alone, though, but ordinary mortals

Like Tommy Kerton and Dan Fraher; Tommy with his
Whitechurch lettuces; Dan with those sensational sweet peas –
I summon these companions, persons who accept what I do
So inappropriately late in the year, the dead and genteel
Who would go to the end of a drill in any December
As they did go to the end of many a winter's drill. But you,

Unsettled ghost of the barely uprooted poem, you fret as much
As two dogs left out in the rain, though I move the bushes
In my bloody-minded manner, on my own, answering to no one.

So, follow me through the slush of still being alive. Mind
These indentations I've left in the scagliola of hardened soil.

When this wayward shrag fell upon my father's head
There was barely a sound in Belleville wood:
The least of the squirrels were hardly impressed
By my father's tree-felling, his quiet mansuetude
That left him the last called, the first dismissed.
What was wild in trees couldn't have understood

The physics of such work, a fall miscalculated,
One worker trepanned of his meek inheritance.
Squirrels watched the leaves falling, the whiplash
Of one dangerous larch coming to grief: it was his head
And not their brainless skulls that timber glanced
Against. I turned and saw the canopy crash

From the shelter of my mother's womb:
Spent ropes were spotted, stained with pitch,
And my father trapped by the tree's overpoise.
Years hence my mother would pick the oakum
From his Post Office book, straining to salvage
Money from loose fibres, muffling her rare cries

In the chainsaw's anisotropic ruthlessness.
Stirred by such a heartless judgement of trees,
She had sallied forth from our cauterised house
To find his falcated frame beneath a wet canopy;
His head as exposed as pilcorn with its faithless glume,
And I, their lone tirailleur, leaping in her womb.

Buoyed by the four new science books in my satchel,
Glossy books just arrived from Library HQ in Lismore,

I skip past the haunted gates of Sir Richard's house.
I am science-rich and spirit-lacking

In this atheistic neighbourhood of 1964:
There is Fermi in my head and a hydrogen bomb.

The army of the night has mounting losses
As I turn the key and open the new-glossed door

Only to come upon my grandmother and Mrs Nagle,
Swapping ghost stories in the November gloom.

The fire has gone out but they haven't noticed.
They are just at that point where Mrs Nagle's husband,

A boy controlling a startled colt, is stared at by the ghost
Of a woman in a dark green tunic. West Waterford, a moonlit road:

Her husband broke a wrist while listening to the dead speak
So now I leave the light on, not to read but to sleep.

Well, I do remember that morning
when your letter clacked onto the sunlit floor
of John Montague's house. We had been
marvelling at our first sight of a Gallimard
Pléiade edition; that loveliness
out of Paris, its 1960s velvet slipcase.

Your poem on the floor was a violation
of sorts, an unwelcome welcome reminder
that air is made of salt. And water –
that gives up everything to the world of paper –
is also a thriving element. We prised
your oyster open, mindful of the sea

in Evelyn's eyes: Mrs Montague, so young
and beautiful in her French sunlight
(to be born beautiful is a glut of privilege) –
It was not that flowers on the window withered
as John flattened your new poem on the table,
but the redress we felt, that sting of brine.

The clock strikes noon on a day of unnaturally heavy rain.
It's moral to stay indoors, to stay out of it, but as usual I'm
Temporising at the edge of an unwritten, bone-dry page.
Truth is, an affair has neither ended to celebrate, nor begun,
To make our poor poetic hearts sick with worries.
The estrangements I feel are the ordinary ones
Of a man who has made few close friends, except
The memory of friendships like distant wars, wars of
Hurried meetings and long betrayals when we were
All so intense, and so very young. The house shudders in rain
And wind, a wind unexpectedly hostile in mid-July.
But the cold outside reminds me yet again how
The brightest and biggest-hearted poets have a genius
For friendship though the page before them is wet and cold:
Something about them draws us out, as if, from our bone-dry
Chairs, the clock striking, we rise to be drenched by rain.

Early April suddenly ablaze and unexpected pear blossom
As rampant as de Chardin's sudden forms of life, as
Delicate as the lacquerwork left over from a raid
Of winter that scattered so many things since autumn –
You could hardly fathom what April brought in on the breeze,
What organic matter-of-fact things, what impolite cascade
Of broken crockery in pink and green. It's like that election
Heard in the distance, beyond the fat privet hedge,
An election that has even set the traffic lights on edge
And caused this collision of ideas. From our quiet section
I can hear anxieties rolling in. But are these not the same as last
Time? Is she not the same? And he, is he not like a gardener
Gone berserk, flat cap askew, trying to make regular
What swarms. Life itself, that is, now swarming on the grass.

THE LAST ARCHITECT IN THE IRISH
PUBLIC SERVICE

The Stygian Council told me to draw a door
But I had to ask them what that was for

When no one would be left in this particular
Drawing office or its marble corridor.

They said an architect could hardly refuse
To draw a closure around the Malton views

Of old Dublin. But I could choose,
They said, between a door as soft as spruce

Or a classic mahogany one. It should be
A simple rectangle, a nod to antiquity;

A door proud to have once been a tree
But happy with change management. See,

They said, how God in Heaven is now
A smaller version of our selves, see how

A hallowed service is emptied. This will allow
Our earthly private realm to grow again. You know

That all of knowledge is but a toll road;
The highway-builders must receive what is owed:

What you built is now cross-hatched and shadowed.
So, draw us an earthly door with electronic code.

Acknowledgements are due to the editors and publishers of the following: RTE Radio One, *The Irish Times*, *The Irish Independent* (*Culture Magazine*), *Irish Examiner*, *Cork Literary Review*, *Manchester Review*, *London Magazine*, *PN Review*, *Plume* (online), *The Poetry Review*, *Poetry Ireland Review*, *Quarryman* (University College, Cork), *The Shop*, *Park* (Berlin), *Poetry International* (Rotterdam), *Times Literary Supplement*, *The Wake Forest Series of Irish Poetry: Volume II* (Wake Forest University Press, 2010).

The author acknowledges with gratitude the support of the Irish Arts Council through its continuing support and advocacy of *Aosdána*, the affiliation of artists in Ireland.